THE ROYAL PALACE,
MADRID

Editorial Everest, S. A., wish to thank all members of the National Heritage who have so kindly collaborated in the production of this book.

Translation: Susan Gosling

Photographs: The National Heritage
Francisco Díez
Everest archives

Layout: Gerardo Rodera

© EDITORIAL EVEREST, S. A.
Carretera León-La Coruña, km 5 - LEÓN
ISBN: 84-241-3940-2
Depósito legal: LE 318-1993
Printed in Spain

EDITORIAL EVERGRÁFICAS, S. L.
Carretera León-La Coruña, km 5
LEÓN (España)

THE ROYAL PALACE, MADRID

FERNANDO CHUECA GOITIA

EDITORIAL EVEREST, S. A.

MADRID • LEON • BARCELONA • SEVILLA • GRANADA • VALENCIA
ZARAGOZA • LAS PALMAS DE GRAN CANARIA • LA CORUÑA
PALMA DE MALLORCA • ALICANTE – MEXICO • BUENOS AIRES

THE ROYAL PALACE, MADRID

AN OLD CASTLE WHICH BECAME
A NEW PALACE

The chronicles tell how on the night of 24th December 1734 a dreadful fire burnt down Madrid Castle, the palace of the kings of the House of Austria.

It is difficult to confirm whether this fire led to its complete and total destruction or whether it was a relative (although quite considerable) destruction, from which certain pieces of ramparts, columned courtyards, towers and walls might remain. This would be extremely arduous to investigate and to clarify for certain. It is very unusual for buildings to be completely destroyed. Roofs and coffered ceilings might go up in flames, as might wooden floors, doors and everything else that is highly inflammable, but there are other things which very rarely perish entirely, and the former castle of the House of Austria may well be included in this category of buildings which are not completely destroyed.

What in fact happened was that as there was a new dynasty ruling Spain, a house of French origin, from a completely different cultural background to that of our monarchs of the House of Hapsburg, Felipe V and his councillors took advantage of this apparently providential destruction to demolish what remained of the former castle to make room for a new one, built to his own taste and that of his times. Who knows if this is true or not?

The demolition of the castle almost completely removed any remains of the former building, which to all intents and purposes became a lost monument. Recently a number of researchers have become very interested in the documental reconstruction of this old building, but we are not here to discuss that enterprise, rather to investigate the new Royal Palace in Madrid, created by the House of Bourbon.[1]

---

[1] The former castle has been studied by Véronique Gerard, a French researcher who has carried out a detailed, highly documented study of this building in her book *De Castillo a palacio: Alcázar de Madrid en el siglo XVI*. Later, the young architect José Barbeiro wrote his doctoral thesis (not yet published) on the castle. This work, for which I had the honour of being consulted, offers a great many details, not only relating to the 16th century, but also up to the moment of the fire in 1734.

1. *Model of the former castle in the Madrid Municipal Museum.*

After the fire Felipe V immediately set to beginning the new palace, which was to symbolise the new state. To carry out this highly compromising and significant enterprise he chose a universally known architect, who could well be considered the most famous of the followers of Vitrubio in the early 18th century. This man was none other than Filippo Juvara. The ambassador of Spain in Rome, Cardinal Acquaviva, immediately contacted the architect, who was in the employ of the court of Savoy, in Turin. Juvara was not originally from Piamonte, but from the other end of Italy, from Messina, in Sicily. But his formation, the beginning of his career, had taken place in Rome, for which reason he is included in the twilight of Roman baroque. Having studied in this excellent school, he later carried out important works in the court of Piamonte, until he became the *Chief Architect* of Savoy.

Juvara arrived in Madrid in the year 1735, that is immediately after the fire in the former castle, and began to work —making designs, choosing a good position, and dedicating all his energy to the great project in hand. But as man proposes yet God disposes, very little life was left to Juvara after his arrival in Madrid. He was not able to live in our fine city for a whole year. On 31st January 1736 this master from Messina suddenly died. Some claimed that it was the treacherous wind from the Guadarrama that finished with his life —neither in his sunny native Sicily, nor in Rome, nor even in the northern town of Turin had Juvara ever experienced such dry, traitorous cold weather. Whether this was the reason or not, what can be affirmed is that this fine architect died and was buried in Madrid, in the former church of San Martín.

There should be some kind of monument —a stele or a monolith— in the city in memory of this great artist who lies to rest in the capital of Spain.

Filippo Juvara imagined a huge palace, which would, no doubt, have been the largest in the whole of Europe. It would, no doubt, have been the largest in the whole of Europe. It would have had four enormous courtyards, one of them open on one side, as a *cour d'honneur* or parade square. This project would obviously not have fitted into the rather small space of the former castle of the House of Austria, which is situated atop a steep slope down to the River Manzanares. The idea of the huge construction which Juvara intended to carry out on the hills of San Barnardino, later used for the Montaña Barracks, and now the Debod Temple Park, had to be abandoned. But it is understandable that the king insisted on the new building being constructed over the ashes of the former. Temples, castles, buildings of religious or political importance have throughout history been placed on specially appointed sites. If the monarchs of Spain had been living in the former castle since the times of the Reconquest, and, in particular, since the times of Felipe II, this place had its own particular charisma, which could not be ignored. There are historic, political and almost mythical reasons which go beyond architecture. With the proposed siting rejected and the architect dead, all the projects varied. But the historic position had been decided on, and as there was no longer Juvara, Giovanni Bautista Sachetti, born in Turin and a follower of Juvara, was summoned.

For this reason it could be wondered whether the present palace shows some vestiges of the style and genius of Juvara. The answer would be affirmative, that it does show something,

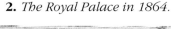

2. *The Royal Palace in 1864.*

3. *The Parade Square and main façade (Photograph by courtesy of the National Heritage).*

even though the layout and the size of Sachetti's new project were smaller. What remains is the order of the façades, proposed by Juvara and retained by Sachetti. These façades are designed in Bernini style, in the baroque-classicist style of the great Napolitan architect and sculptor.

This Bernini style, which the architect also used in Odescalchi Palace and in his plans for the renovation of the Louvre in Paris, is as follows: the base is a bolster, which forms a great pedestal for the building, and a row of pillars, which may be columns or pilasters, rising up from the pedestal. These pillars are enormous, and at least two storeys high. This has become known as *gigantic style*. Above these is an entablature, then a classical balustrade with pedestals on which stand sculpted figures, urns, torches and other decorative pieces. The project designed by Juvara was followed precisely by Sachetti, but as the latter had to limit himself to a reduced ground plan he had to increase the number of floors in the palace without spoiling the three fundamental ones, which he did by resorting to the insertion of *mezzanines* or entresols. Sachetti carried out this task magnificently and the result is splendid façades which are fine examples of the vitality and beauty of 18th century architecture. The memory of Juvara and his project can also be appreciated in the courtyards, staircases and other rooms, since this disciple always revered his master.

4. Window on the main façade.

5. Detail of the east façade.

9

The large courtyard, the only one that remains of the four projected by Juvara, would also have satisfied the first architect because of its design and dignity. The most obvious precedent of this courtyard is perhaps that in the palace of the Duke of Modena, by the architect Avanzini.

The first stone of the new palace was laid on 7th April 1738. The decisions were quite clearly taken quickly, as only four years elapsed between the fire in the castle in 1734, through Juvara's projects, presented in 1736, and the laying of the first stone in 1738. But while the organisation was very rapid, the actual construction of the palace took many years, possibly more than anybody imagined. It was not finished and accomodated for living in until 1764, during the reign of Carlos III. Neither Felipe V, who reigned for many years, nor Fernando VI could take up residence there. It took twenty-six years to be completed, and even then many things were left for the future.

Giovanni Bautista Sachetti had a fine assistant in Ventura Rodríguez, an exceptional young architect from Madrid. He did not merely help, but really collaborated with Sachetti, so that various examples of his talent can be appreciated in numerous parts of the building.

6. *The north façade by night. (Photograph by courtesy of the National Heritage).*

7. *View of the palace from Oriente Square.
In the foreground, a statue of Felipe IV.*

ORGANISATION OF THE BUILDING

The palace in Madrid can be said to be one of the strongest, most powerful and most solid built by man. It is really colossal —the best way to define it would be as a «mass». Very few buildings in the world can be considered as such. For example, the monastery of El Escorial is an immense, magnificent building, which is larger and of greater dimensions than the Royal Palace in Madrid. It has many courtyards, corridors and different rooms, a church that is majestic, towers, belfries and spires. As a whole it is absolutely breathtaking, but it is not a mass. A mass is something far more compact, closed and colossal. The Royal Palace in Madrid is one, and certain palaces in Italy could also possibly be described as such.

The Farnese Palace in Rome, Caprarola Castle in Vignola and, perhaps, Caserta Palace near Naples could also qualify. But most of the other palaces throughout Europe —the Louvre in Paris, Versailles, Schönbrunn, the great palaces in Germany— are different; they are huge palaces which are far more open than this in Madrid. Some of these strong, solid castles also have a certain military touch. This is to be found in the Royal Palace too, where an attempt has been made to commemorate the castle of the House of Austria in the square layout with its four towers.

This compact, solid palace stands on a hill overlooking the valley of the Manzanares. Its north façade has the

8. *Aerial view of the palace. (Photograph by courtesy of Paisajes Españoles).* ▶

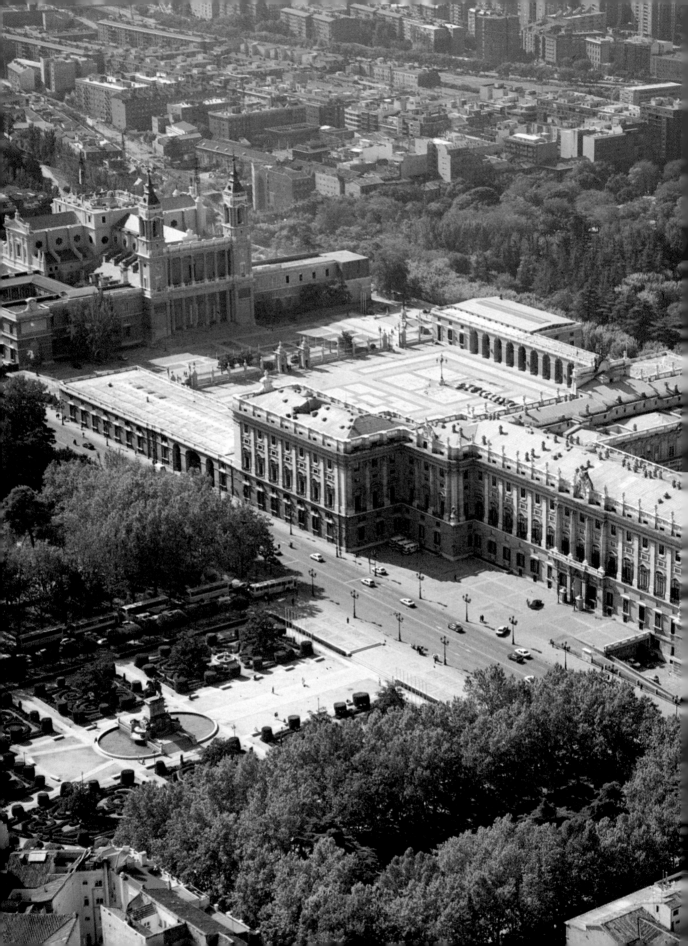

appearance of a strong, doughty castle, as does the west façade, although this to a lesser extent than the north façade, which stands firm upon several terraces and foundations.

The distribution of the palace also corresponds to its compact, solid layout. One single, perfectly square courtyard of great dimensions, around which the whole is organised, gives light to the building.

There are two corridors from this courtyard to the façades. The main one, which is wider, has windows to

14

the street. The interior one, which is narrower and contains some offices, has windows to the courtyard. As mentioned above, the layout is simple, based on concentric squares. On the north and south sides the interior corridor is wider —on the south because of the fine staircase and the Columns Room, and on the north because of the great palatial chapel.

The main rooms are, naturally, placed along the exterior corridor, which gi-

As can be appreciated, this palace, unlike the other great palaces in Europe, has not been prepared with great, spectacular rooms. It has already been mentioned that three rooms on the west side had to be joined, using highly decorated arches, in order to create a banqueting room. The Throne Room is an exception. Although not very large, it is dignified and magnificent because of its artistic beauty and wealth.

11. *The terrace over the main courtyard.*

ves to the street. There are seven rooms on the south side, the most important —the Throne Room— being in the centre. There are another seven rooms on the west side, but three of these have been joined to make up the Banqueting Room. The smallest rooms are on the north side, as the greater part of this is taken up by the chapel. Seven rooms are distributed between the towers on the east side. All these rooms are, of course, situated on the main floor since they are the most important.

The only fairly large room is the Columns Room, which is such because Sabatini turned the double staircase planned by Sachetti into a single one.

All these details refer to the main floor, the important floor from the points of view of both art and protocol. The remaining floors generally follow the same distribution based on two concentric squares, except in the part housing the chapel, and the staircase with the Columns Room, which take up the full height of the building.

15

12. *The Parade Square.*

THE ROYAL PALACE
AS A SYMBOL AND ALLEGORY.

The kings of Spain wanted one of their many palaces to be not only a royal residence, the throne from which they would exercise their power and the setting for their ceremonial acts and receptions, but also a symbolic monument in which the magnificence and splendour of the Spanish monarchy could be made evident through its works of art.

The Bourbons were generous, for they did not limit themselves to exalting the new dynasty, their own, but they also elevated the varied tradition to which they felt closely related. Sculpture and painting were the main means of this exaltation.

The next section will be dedicated to the symbolic decorative sculpture. Then,

13. *Detail of the façade, from the parade square.*

14. *Detail of the façade from the parade square.*

with the description of the rooms in the palace, will come a description of the magnificent «al fresco» paintings in the vaults, which depict the triumphs and grandeur of the Spanish monarchy in allegorical form.

Sculpture plays a very important part in the decoration of the four façades, and was of great interest to the architect Sachetti and the sculptor Juan Domingo Oliveri right from 1742. But the person really responsible for the organisation of the iconographic series was Father Martín Sarmiento, a learned Benedictine from Pontevedra, who belonged to the school of Father Feijóo and carried out praiseworthy work, mainly evident in the large statues on pedestals along the balustrade which crown the palace, in the single statues at corners and other suitable points, in the coats-of-arms, in the relief work and allegorical panels, and, in particular, in the marble work above the doors in the gallery on the main floor. Father Sarmiento took care of all this with a criterion based on the fundamental, but varying the decorations as the building grew and developed.

There is no room here to analyse iconographic development. It is explained in the exhaustive study by Francisco Javier de la Plaza[2], which gives a full account of the complexity and transcendency of the subject.

Plaza has drawn up a list of the pieces of sculpture, beginning with Ataulfo and ending with Luis I. There are ninety statues apart from those of Ferdinand VI, Barbara of Braganza and María-Louisa of Savoy, situated at the top of the south façade. They were made by the best sculptors of the time, such as Felipe de Castro, Domingo Olivieri, A. Dumandré, Juan Pascual de Mena, Roberto Michel, Manuel Álvarez, Juan de Villanueva (the father of the famous architect) and Salvador Carmona. The most represented are Juan Domingo Olivieri and Felipe de Castro, who were directors of the San Fernando Royal Academy and oracles of sculpture during the reigns of Felipe V and Fernando VI. As well as our own monarchs, there are also statues of the four Roman emperors born in Spain —Arcadius, Trajan, Teodosius and Honorius— who have also changed places in the statue dance which the Spanish so enjoy. Those who have returned to their places are Moctezuma and Atahualpa, the chosen from among the kings of the Spanish Empire, which was widened by our possessions overseas.

Very strange is the case of the marble relief work above the niches in the main gallery of the palace. These niches, one of Sachetti's typical designs, had above the doors medallions of mixtilineal outline which were to be decorated with relief work alluding to the history of Spain, arranged in four groups, in accordance with the four galleries in the courtyard.

On the south, the Throne Room side, would be the medallions from the political group. On the north, the Chapel side, would be those on a religious theme, on the east side those of a military nature, and on the west side the cultural and scientific ones. On each side, or gallery, there are eleven pieces of relief work by artists such as Juan Domingo Olivieri, Manuel Álvarez, Juan de Mena, Michel, Dumandré and so on.

It would be marvellous to see this work in the correct position completing the doors, which are of an extremely unusual design. Among those on the religious theme we could contemplate the placing of the chasuble on St. Ildefonso,

---
[2] *El Palacio Real Nuevo de Madrid,* Francisco-Javier de la Plaza, Valladolid, 1975.

15. *Statue of Honorius, in the main courtyard.*

16. *Statue of Teodosius, in the main courtyard.*

or the III Council of Toledo; among the military ones the conquest of Seville, or that of Mexico; among the political ones the Council of State or the proclamation of the Seven Laws; among the cultural ones Nebrija's *Gramática,* or the edition of the *Biblia Complutense.*

But all this has wandered like a flock with no shepherd and each piece of work has followed its own path. Some are now housed in the Prado Museum and others in the San Fernando Academy of Fine Arts. It would not be difficult to return them to their original places, and the palace would regain a valuable part of its splendour.

But why did this inconceivable looting take place? What led to this flight of statues, images, relief work, history and allegory? The reason is that there are simple yet destructive changes in fashion and taste. This royal palace was first designed according to the tastes of late baroque, which under Juvara had flourished in Turin and Piamonte, and which did not expect to meet up halfway with severe neoclassicism and its

archaeological pedantry. At this difficult yet critical moment Carlos III arrived in Madrid (1759) and this restorer of Pompeii was inculcated with archaising ideas, which conflicted with the baroque style, albeit very gradually and courteously. He was intoxicated by Mengs, the painter from Bohemia who was known as the *philosopher artist.* Carlos III, who possessed the virtue of asking the learned for their advice, made a mistake on this occasion. He had every faith in Mengs, who advised him to avoid all showiness, finery and other adornments in the palace, as he considered them improper to the severity of an exclusive classicism. But although the palace still remained as it was, it lost many magnificent pieces which ornamented it and made of it, moreover, the symbol and message of a great idea called Spain. To Carlos III, who was so just and prudent in everything, and to his artistic oracle we owe this outrage; attempts have been made to correct this over the last few years, but they have been timid and lacked real decision.

THE ROYAL PALACE, MADRID

MAIN FLOOR

1. Main staircase.
2. Halberdiers Room.
3. Columns Room.
4. Gasparini Waiting Room.
5. Gasparini Antechamber.
6. Gasparini Room.
7. Carlos III Corridor.
8. Carlos III Room.
9. Porcelain Room.
10. Yellow Room.
11. Banqueting Room.
12. Exhibition Rooms.
13. Reliquary.
14. Royal Chapel.
15. Queen Christina Rooms.
16. Queen Christina Antechamber.
17. Anteroom.
18. Queen Cristina Waiting Room.
19. Dining Room.
20. Mirrors Room.
21. Tapestries Room.
22. Arms Room.
23. Corridor.
24. Chamber.
25. Antechamber.
26. Waiting Room.
27. Throne Room.
28. Grandees Room.
29. Tapestries Room.
30. Fine Works Room.
31. Stucco Room.
32. Chinese-Japanese Room.
33. Billiard Room.

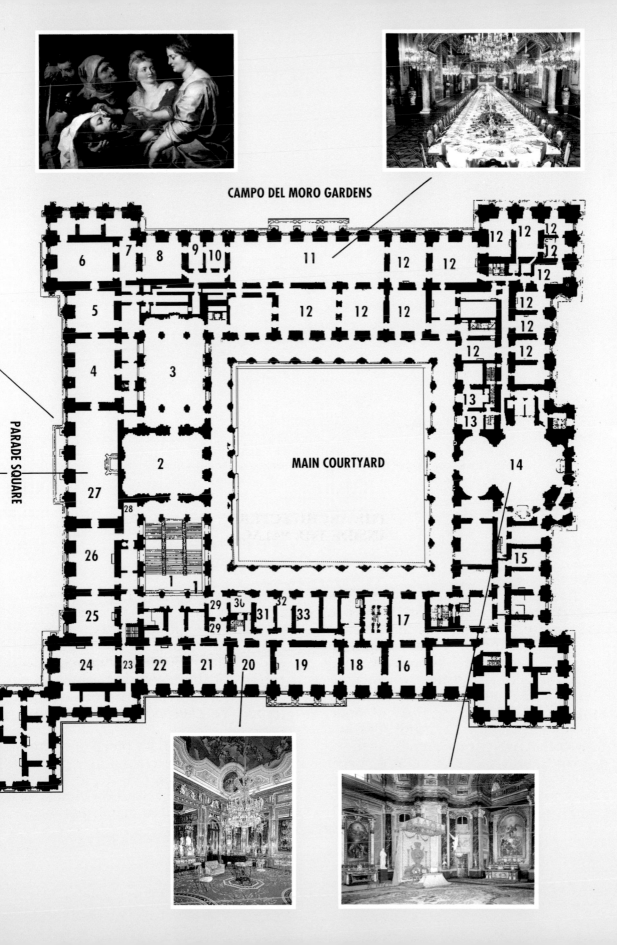

CAMPO DEL MORO GARDENS

PARADE SQUARE

MAIN COURTYARD

17. *The Royal Chapel (Photograph by courtesy of the National Heritage).*

THE ARCHITECTURE
INSIDE THE PALACE

As well as the characteristics of the exterior of the palace referred to above, which are in the style of the architect Bernini, there is an equally important interior style of architecture. We shall begin with the courtyard, which is perfectly square and extremely similar to that of the palace of the Duke of Modena, by the architect Avanzini. Two storeys of archways make up the main ordinance, and above this double loggia is a top floor which is sufficiently set back to give the courtyard more light.

This courtyard has an extremely important function —that of ensuring movement around the whole building and its most important rooms. On the main floor it serves as a processional gallery and it was generally used in the important religious celebrations of the court, for ceremonies which naturally finished in the chapel: *Te Deums,* baptisms, funerals, etc.

The most important piece of interior architecture is the chapel itself, a fine church which compensates its rather small dimensions with the richness of its decoration and its manificent materials.

18. *Altar in the Royal Chapel (Photograph by courtesy of the National Heritage).*

19. *The Reliquary (Photograph by courtesy of the National Heritage).*

23

The chapel has an eliptic ground plan and faces from east to west. It has a prolongation corresponding to the high altar at one end and the smaller choir at the other. It also has a kind of entrance or atrium joined to the central layout of the church, as well as two high altars. It is crowned by a beautiful circular cupola illuminated by four large circular windows at the four points of the compass. This cupola was magnificently painted *al fresco* to represent heavenly glory by Corrado Giaquinto, between 1753 and 1762. One of the vaults was possibly painted first. The architecture of the chapel naturally corresponds to the main architect Giovanni Bautista Fachetti, but it is widely considered that the Spanish architect Ventura Rodríguez played a decisive role in the project.

As mentioned above, Ventura Rodríguez had been working as a prominent draughtsman since work on the new palace had begun, but as the work advanced he had gained more prestige and authority. Certain characteristics of this chapel, such as the great flared arches decorated with classical coffered ceilings, are very typical of the architecture of Ventura. Many similar ones can be seen in the church of San Marcos in Madrid, one of the earliest works by this architect from Ciempozuelos.

The magnificent, splendid chapel with its frescoes by Giaquito, its St. Michael the Archangel by Ramón Bayeu on the high altar, lamps by M. Águeda, beautiful organ by Boch, daises, canopies, stucco and relief work, carpets and candelabra is truly breathtaking. A more severe note amongst such magnificence is struck by the shafts in black Mariñaria marble of the Corinthian columns.

Close to the chapel, but not open to the public, is the magnificent *reliquary* in fine woods, which dates from the time of Fernando VII. The relief by Alejandro Algardi is small, but is an example of the pomposity of Roman baroque.

There is still an excellent piece of religious architecture in the Royal Palace. Not open to the public and half-hidden on the second floor, this is known as the Ladies-in-Waiting Chapel, since in this part lived the more important members of the female staff.

It is a beautiful chapel, oval in shape but curved between the corners and the windows so that it widens almost to a square. The layout could be by Sachetti, but the decoration appears to be later. The ceiling and a painting at the altar, a Virgin Mary, are by Maella[3].

Another important part of the interior architecture is that of the great staircase together with its vestibules, landings and adjoining rooms.

On the ground floor the entrance to the palace is extremely solemn, through a noble portico worked in stone, with pilasters standing together with Tuscan columns —extremely typical of Sachetti's work. The portico leads through a passageway to the great staircase, opposite which a niche houses a statue of Carlos III dressed as a Roman, with a short tunic, a cuirass and a mantle, in marble, by the French sculptor Pierre de Michel.

The great staircase shows real *architectural bravado* and appears to be a

---

[3] José Luis Sancho has published a photograph of this chapel in a highly-documented article called, "El Palacio Real de Madrid, Alternativas y Críticas a un Proyecto", *Revista Reales Sitios,* Special edition, 1989.

20. *Statue of Carlos III.*

21. *Portico (Photograph by courtesy of the National Heritage).*

magnificent piece of scenery from an opera. This is a recomposition by Saba-tini on a project already begun by Sa-chetti. The latter had a main staircase twice the width of the present one, with two spaces, or symmetrical stairwells, one at either side of the main entrance to the palace. As it is simpler, Sabatini's staircase may well be more solemn, but it has lost the magnificence of the shape of a double staircase.

The great height of the stairwell of-fers this space a special grandeur —the enormous circular windows, or bull's eyes, giving light to the fine vault, the general elegance of the tone, the gilt mirrors with candelabra, the garlands and golden frames and, above all, the frescoes by Corrado Giaquinto, repre-

senting the triumph of religion and the Church, place this staircase among the best of 18th century Italian architecture. It has been said that this staircase is mo-delled on that in Caserta Palace, built by Vanvitelli for Carlos III when he was King of Naples, but this is only a vague approximation.

The staircase leads directly to the Halberdiers' Room, which was where the two staircases envisaged by Sachetti were to meet. As a result of these trans-formations, the Halberdiers or Guards Room is cold and colourless when compared with the opulence of the staircase. Walls with flattish pillasters support an entablature from which rises a vault with prominent plaster borders. It is decorated with a series of 18th and

22. *Vault over the main staircase. «The Triumph of Religion and the Church», by Corrado Giaquinto. (Photograph by courtesy of the National Heritage).*

23. *Main staircase (Photograph by courtesy of the National Heritage).* ▶

24. *Bronze statue
in the Columns Room.*

19th century adornments by Dessert, magnificent console tables, and paintings by Lucas Jordán and Martínez del Mazo.

The most attractive part of this severe room is the ceiling, by Giovanni Bautista Tiepolo, but unsigned, as are all his works. This great painter is the standard-bearer of 18th century painting in his magnificent native city of Venice. As before him had been Titian, Tintoretto and Veronés. The pictorial scenography unfurled by Tiepolo on the ceilings and architectural settings of the finest palaces in Europe cannot be equalled. Born in Venice in 1696, he died in Madrid in 1770. He was summoned to our city in 1762 by Carlos III and spent eight years of his maturity working hard among us, having lost none of the drive of youth. He came accompanied by his sons Giovanni Domenico and Lorenzo.

25. *The Columns Room (Photograph by courtesy of the National Heritage).*

After the ceiling in the Throne Room, the next best in the palace is that in the Halberdiers Room, which represents the *Apotheosis of Aeneas,* told by Virgil. The chiaro-oscuro work is really beautiful —porcelain-like clouds and skies of pale transparent blue compose a masterly symphony.

The following room is the Columns Room, a result of the supression of the symmetric staircases projected by Sachetti. This is a very large room with a proportioned height identical to the well of the single staircase. Because it was so big, the Columns Room was used for balls and great receptions up to the death of Queen Mercedes. Here

27. *The Halberdiers Room.*

26. *The ceiling in the Halberdiers Room.*

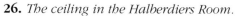

was held the «Washing and Feeding of the Poor» on Maundy Thursday; here General Franco lay in state; here, many years later, on 12th June 1985, the agreement by which Spain became a member of the European Economic Community was signed on the table of bronze and stone called *De las Esfinges.*

This table was designed by Percier, an architect of Napoleon Bonaparte's, and made by the bronze-worker Thomire. It is significant that an act of the unification of Europe should have taken place on a table in the *imperial style* of a man who dreamed of uniting Europe.

Tapestries depicting the Acts of the Apostles and bronzelike statues, a legacy from the prince cardinal to Felipe IV to be used to decorate the Buen Retiro Palace, adorn the solemn architecture, all under the gaze of Carlos V dominating Rage, a copy of the famous statue by León Leoni now in the Prado Museum.

This ceiling is another of the most highly esteemed in the palace. It represents the birth of the sun, and is by Corrado Giaquinto, a painter of the Napolitan School (1699-1750) and a follower of Francisco Solimena. It can certainly be claimed that Tiepolo and Giaquinto are the two greatest fresco painters in this palace. Because of their elegant baroque style, their vigour and decorative eloquence and their special way of organising mythology they surpass all others. Each of them has his own untransferable personality; they are not interchangeable, but they both harmonise with the spirit of the palace in an admirable way. This ceiling by Giaquinto depicting the birth of the sun is as invaluable as that over the main staircase and that on the cupola of the chapel.

Both of them were succeeded by the artist Mengs, who was to become Carlos III's favourite painter. Mengs, born in Aussing in Bohemia and known as the *philosopher painter,* was celebrated by the learned and for this reason won himself great esteem in the court. He also gained that of the king, who always allowed himself to be influenced by his ministers and councillors. This painter brought about an artistic revolution which gravely affected the palace. It seems that his was the idea to take away the statues crowning the building, as well as other decorations both in and outside. This was a mistake which still has to be rectified. It has already been mentioned above.

THE THRONE ROOM

This room, also known as the *Kingdoms* Room is, from the hierarchal point of view, the first in the palace. Here is the canopied throne of the Catholic monarchy, and here are held its most representative ceremonies. If it is the first in hierarchal order, it is also the room that arouses most emotion in the visitor from an artistic point of view. Here we should best listen to Paul Guinard, the famous scholar of Spain who until not long ago lived in our country and has left us one of the most beautiful and inspired descriptions of this room, which is radiant in its golds and warm tones of crimson. «The Throne Room», writes Guinard, «which dates from the beginning of the reigh of Carlos III, is an accumulation of extremely considerable riches a marble floor, chandeliers made of cut glass, tall rococo mirrors with their golden frames aligning walls of maroon velvet, Louis XVI console tables on which stand Roman busts and marble clocks alternating with others in bronze. This interplay of dark reds and heavy blacks would be a little sad if it were not for the fresco by Tiepolo, which makes the whole brighter and is the greatest marvel in the palace».

The Venetian painter, who was commissioned to represent the glories of Spain, took care not to overladen the immense ceiling. In the centre is a pale blue sky dotted with light clouds, between which float Cupids and female figures with long trumpets, representing Fame. The main designs are grouped at the sides —Apollo with his lyre on a carriage drawn by sea monsters; young Spain rises up on her throne between Hercules and Minerva; beside them stands Religion dressed in white and half-veiled, offering the chalice and the cross to uncivilised nations; a choir of young women surrounds the obelisk proclaiming the glory of Carlos III, the *Magnanimous*. But around the edges of the ceiling Tiepolo amuses himself. The retinue of the provinces of Spain and other parts of the world serve as a pretext to his fantasy. On one side there is a caravel, its bowsprit twisted by a storm, full of indians, lions and leopards, which the captain is showing to an amazed old Neptune. On another there are emaciated conquistadors, their banners flying, bringing home captives, and there is a beautiful black woman on a dromedary offering Spain a palm. Languid Asians, indians bristling with feathers, peasants from Galicia driving their oxen, Arab merchants with pointed hats, men from Madrid wrapped in cloaks and two-cornered hats, orange groves and ostriches together with birds of paradise all go to make up an unexpected, delightful carnival. Tiepolo never showed more youthful passion than in this official composition, which was to be his swansong. He died in Madrid in 1770, shortly after completing it.

28. *The Throne Room (Photograph by courtesy of the National Heritage).*

29. *Detail of the Throne Room (Photograph by courtesy of the National Heritage).* ▶

30. *The official chamber.*

OTHER MAIN ROOMS

The following are the other main rooms in the palace.

OFFICIAL CHAMBER. Situated in the southeast corner beside the rooms used by Alfonso XIII and Queen Victoria Eugenia. The walls are covered with brocaded velvet and the vault was painted in 1797 by Mariano Salvador Maella on the theme of the *Apotheosis of Hadrian*. Portraits of Alfonso XII by Casado del Alisal and of Maria Christina of Hapsburg by Moreno Carbonero decorate the walls.

ANTECHAMBER. A room of great beauty with walls in blue, it contains portraits of Ferdinand of Naples and of Alfonso XIII and Victoria Eugenia by Pardiñas and Sotomayor respectively. A round pedestal table in bronze with allegories of the rivers of Spain, a present from England to Ferdinand VIII, stands in the centre of the antechamber.

The vault, painted by Domenici Tiepolo, son of Giovanni Bautista, represents the Golden Fleece.

This is followed by the WAITING ROOM. Unusually, this is larger than the antechamber. All those who asked for an audience with the king were allowed in here. The walls are covered with red damask, and instead of paintings there are tapestries from the Royal Tapestry in Madrid on cartoons similar to those by Teniers.

The vault is magnificent and fascinating, another creation by Giovanni Bautista Tiepolo. The theme is that of *The Power of the Spanish Monarchy*.

31. *Official antechamber.*

32. *Official waiting room.*

33. *Fresco on the vault of the waiting room (Photograph by courtesy of the National Heritage).*

34. *Tapestry of «The Alchemist» in the official waiting room (Photograph by courtesy of the National Heritage).*

36. *Detail of the Gasparini Room (Photograph by courtesy of the National Heritage).*

37. *The Gasparini Room (Photograph by courtesy of the National Heritage)*

Beyond the Throne Room is the GASPARINI WAITING ROOM, where Carlos III would have lunch. The decoration here was completely changed in the 19th century. The vault, painted by Mengs, represents the *Apotheosis of Trajan.* Several paintings by Lucas Jordán and very ostentatious lamps in bronze and glass give this room a touch of special majesty.

Carlos III would have supper and hold conversations in the GASPARINI ANTECHAMBER. Here there were paintings by Velázquez —equestrian portraits of Felipe III and Felipe IV with their wives, and one of the Count of Olivares— as well as that of Carlos V in Mühlberg by Titian. Now, there are portraits of Carlos IV and Maria Luisa, by Goya, and busts by Juan Adán.

An enormous clock representing Chronos, by Luis Godó, a large French chandelier in bronze and glass, candelabra and other equally valuable objects give a certain glory to this room, in which Mengs painted the *Apotheosis of Hercules.*

The final room on the main (south) façade is the famous GASPARINI ROOM, one of the most beautiful and interesting creations in the palace. Here Carlos III would dress, assisted by his gentlemen-in-waiting, and in the presence of the Court. The decoration from the times of this great king has been maintained entirely.

Gasparini was an artist who came to Madrid from Naples expressly to decorate the king's room in 1760. He completed it in 1774. The decoration is presumptuous and very original —typical of an exhuberant Napolitan.

It is very difficult to define his style, which is rococo with elements of «chinoiserie», and surpasses the wild fantasies of the Oppenords and Meissonier. The silks covering the walls were embroidered by José Canops after designs by Gasparini; also his are the designs on the original marble flooring. If we had to find something similar to this Napolitan's art it would be that of Hipólito Rovira, from Valencia, who built the Marquis of Dos Aguas' palace in Valencia. Rovira, who died in 1765, was almost a contempory of Gasparini's.

The corridor known as Carlos III's, which houses Goya's cartoon *The Wild Boar Hunt* and portraits of James III of England and Juan V of Portugal by Taviani and J. Rank respectively, leads to the CARLOS III ROOM, which was the

40. *The Porcelain Room (Photograph by courtesy of the National Heritage).*

room where this king died on 14th December 1788. After this death, Fernando VII had the room decorated, placing on the walls silk dotted with stars, with a border showing the emblem of the Order of Carlos III. Dominating the room is a portrait of the king, dressed in the clothes of the order he created, by Mariano Salvador Maella (1784). The vault was painted by Vicente López in 1828.

The Porcelain Room leads to the YELLOW ROOM, which is richly fitted out with tapestries, furniture in various styles, lamps and carpets, and serves as an ante-room to the BANQUETING ROOM. This is made up of three rooms of what were known as the *Queen María Amelia of Saxony's Quarters.*

It was created by Alfonso XII on the occasion of his second marriage, to Ma-

41. *Yellow room (Photograph by courtesy of the National Heritage).*

The following room is the PORCELAIN ROOM (1765-1770) with pieces from the Buen Retiro Works, by José Gricci and the painters Jenaro Boltri and Juan Bautista de la Torre, who were also responsible for the Porcelain Room in Aranjuez.

ria Christina of Hapsburg and Lorraine. 16th century tapestries from Brussels (*The Story of Vertumnus and Pomona,* by Wilhelm Panemaker) decorate the wall casings. The first vault is by Mengs, the second by Antonio González and the last by Francisco Bayeu.

42. The Banqueting Room (Photograph by courtesy of the National Heritage).

44

43. *«The Surrender of Granada», fresco by Francisco Bayeu in the Banqueting Room (Photograph by courtesy of the National Heritage).*

The first represents Dawn, the second Christopher Columbus before King Ferdinand and Queen Isabella and the third the surrender of Granada. It should be remembered that this was once three separate rooms which have been cleverly joined by means of wide arches.

The room is lit by fifteen chandeliers in cut glass and bronze together with ten matching wall lamps, which fill the room with great splendour and magnificence during ceremonial meals. Beyond the Banqueting Room there is an exhitibion of the palace silver.

Further on, and now in the northwest tower, there is a series of rooms and waiting rooms, all quite small, which housed the palace collection of art, now dispersed around the building. Some pieces, such as a portrait of Felipe *the Good,* Duke of Burgundy, by Van der Weyden, and a Bosco showing the Road to Calvary, are first class.

Various works attributed to Bassano and others by the prolific Lucas Jordán, together with a *St. Paul* by El Greco, are all worthy of mention. There are also pieces by Velázquez, such as a white horse which is a study for a portrait of the Count of Olivares, and the head of this favourite of Felipe IV's in a small square, almost a miniature. An equestrian portrait of Juan of Austria, by Ribera, is an exceptional piece of work. Magnificent portraits of Felipe IV and Isabel of Bourbon, by Rubens, show the supremacy of this painter who was closely linked to the court of Spain.

There are some examples of the religious painting of Mengs, while those of customs demonstrate the talent of Tiepolo. The palace houses two pictures by Watteau, a painter who is hardly represented in Spanish colections. By Goya, there are the portraits of Carlos IV and María Luisa in the Gasparini Room.

We have not attempted to outline all the works housed in the palace as this, just as if we were to mention all the objects of art here, would lead to a tedious inventory and would make us miss the global evaluation of the monument. The paradox would be like not seeing the wood for the trees.

Moving on clockwise we pass through the chapel, which has already been mentioned, into the rooms used by Christina, the mother of Alfonso XIII. Of interest in the antechamber are the paintings and a late Empire bronze and malachite pedestal table.

In Queen Christina's antechamber there are tapestries from the *Heroes of the Trojan War* series, stitched in Beauvais in the 18th century. As elsewhere, clocks, candelabra, rococo console tables, the carpet and a ceiling painted by Mariano Maella help to enrich the room.

The DINING ROOM is one of the most splendid rooms on the east corridor. It is situated in the centre of the façade that faces in this direction and gives to Oriente Square. The walls are covered with red velvet; the enormous mirrors showing medallions and the architectural decoration give distinction to this room, the largest on the east side. The room is dominated by a large portrait of Queen Isabel II with her daughter, Princess Isabel, painted by Winterhalter in 1865. The vault represents the *Fall of the Giants,* by Francisco Bayeu.

44. *«Columbus before King Ferdinand and Queen Isabella», by Antonio González*
◀ *Velázquez, in the Banqueting Room (Photograph by courtesy of the National Heritage).*

45. *«Felipe the Good», by Van der Weyden
(Photograph by courtesy of the National Heritage).*

46. *«Salome and Herodias
Contemplating the Head
of John the Baptist»,
by Gerard Seghers.
(Photograph by courtesy
of the National Heritage).*

48. *«The Wild Boar Hunt»,
cartoon for a tapestry, by Goya.
(Photograph by courtesy of the
National Heritage).*

47. *«Country Duo»,
by Watteau.*

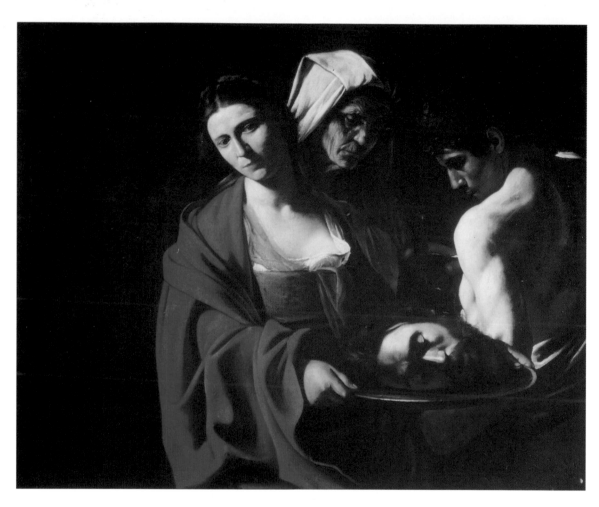

49. *«Salome with the Head of John the Baptist», by Caravaggio.*
(Photograph by courtesy of the National Heritage).

51. *«The Blind Man and his Guide's Meal», by Luis Paret (Photograph by courtesy of the National Heritage).*

50. *«Fernando VII Dressed in the Order of the Golden Fleece», by Vicente López (Photograph by courtesy of the National Heritage).*

53. *The Dining Room (Photograph by courtesy of the National Heritage).*

52. *Queen Maria Christina's Antechamber. (Photograph by courtesy of the National Heritage).*

One of the most original rooms in the palace is the MIRROR ROOM, situated just beside the Dining Room. It first appears to be a porcelain room, because of the colours of the decorations, in which the predominant shade is blue with decorative relief work in white, that is, precisely in the colours of the famous English Wedgewood porcelain, which is so characteristic of the neoclassical period. It is a very Carlos IV room, with a striking bronze and glass chandelier in the shape of a top. The huge porcelain clock from El Retiro, dated 1799, is another in the magnificent collection of clocks in the palace. The large ceramic vases are Sèvres, but because of their colours —blue and white— are similar to Wedgewood.

This room was once Queen Maria Louisa of Parma's dressing room, and later the royal family's conversation and concert room. The only thing that is stylistically different from the neoclassical

54. *Lamp in Queen Maria Christina's Antechamber. (Photograph by courtesy of the National Heritage).*

55. *Detail of the Dining Room (Photograph by courtesy of the National Heritage).*

56. *Fresco on the vault of the Mirrors Room. (Photograph by courtesy of the National Heritage).*

57. *The Mirrors Room (Photograph by courtesy of the National Heritage).*

58. *Detail of the Mirrors Room. (Photograph by courtesy of the National Heritage).*

by Bayeu in 1794. It represents the Orders of the Spanish monarchy: the Golden Fleece, Carlos III and María Luisa, and the military Orders of Santiago, Calatrava, Alcántara and Montesa.

The following room, the *Arms Room,* is different from the majority in the palace, which are examples of rococo and Carlos IV. It is decorated with 17th century tapestries from Brussels showing the story of Scipio, and others with *galleries* and *gardens.* With its wooden socles and Louis XIII armchairs, it looks older than the other rooms, although it is in fact more modern, for while the decoration is 17th century in style it was carried out at the end of the 19th century.

This room houses one of the greatest artistic treasures in the palace —a tryptych composed of a series of small panels which belonged to Queen Isa-

concept of the room is the ceiling painted by Bayeu, which represents Hercules on Mount Olympus.

The following two rooms —the *Tapestry* room and the *Arms Room*— are of a different character. The first has this name because of its large tapestries from the Royal Workshop of Santa Bárbara, stitched by Vandergoten after cartoons by Corrado Giaquinto and José del Castillo, copies of originals by Lucas Jordán and Solimera. Their religious themes are taken from the Old Testament.

The whole room is magnificently furnished, as are all the rooms into the palace, with console tables, candelabra, an enormous chandelier, clocks and pedestal tables. The ceiling was painted

59. *The Mirrors Room. Stucco work above the doors. (Photograph by courtesy of the National Heritage).*

60. *The Tapestry Room. (Photograph by courtesy of the National Heritage).*

61. *The Arms Room (Photograph by courtesy of the National Heritage).*

62. *Two panels of a tryptych by Juan de Flandes. Now in the corridor.*
(Photograph by courtesy of the National Heritage).

bella, attributed to Juan de Flandes and Miguel Sitium. The tryptych is made up of 15 panels, although at the time of Queen Isabella it contained 45. After her death the others were gradually dispersed. Painted circa 1496, these wonderful small panels depict various stages in the life of Christ. Of insuperable serenity, elegance and gentleness, they are a product of that unique moment when mediaeval mysticism met humanistic aestheticism.

The painting on the ceiling, which is within a circle, represents Hercules between Virtue and Vice. The work is in porcelain colours.

Still continuing in a clockwise direction we move on into the Chamber Corridor, with a fine painting by Palmorali, showing Princess Isabel, sister of Alfonso XII, as a young woman.

There are also two fine works by Watteau.

This corridor leads to the chamber, the antechamber and the waiting room, then back to the Throne Room, so that the whole circuit has now been completed.

The chamber also leads to Alfonso XIII and Queen Victoria Eugenia's private rooms, in the southwest wing which was added on by Sabatini, thus breaking the symmetry and leading to a loss of clarity and correspondence in the layout of the palace.

The rooms in the Sabatini wing are smaller than those in the rest of the palace, but not for this do they lack indisputable artistic values, particularly in the *Queen's Suite*. Of great interest, *verbi gratia,* are Queen Victoria Eugenia's reception room, with the portrait of Louis XIV by Rigaud, and the library, the music room and the queen's own bedroom, all pleasant, cheerful rooms. The ceilings were painted by Maella.

Alfonso XII's private rooms, which are not open to the public, are of historic rather than decorative interest, although the king's private office shows a fine neoclassical ceiling by Bayeu. The king's bedroom is impressive in its sobriety and severity. Above the very simple bed hangs a crucifix flanked by two small flags —that of Spain and the king's purple standard.

Also of interest, from a historic point of view, is the COUNCIL ROOM, where the king met with his ministers around a small table, which shows how reduced the aparatus of administration was in those days.

64. *Queen María Christina's waiting room (Photograph by courtesy of the National Heritage).*

63. *Detail of the furniture in Queen Maria Christina's music room. (Photograph by courtesy of the National Heritage).*

In these pages we have dealt with the most important of the many riches within the Royal Palace, although there are, obviously, many others which have been omitted —not only architectural and decorative details, but also countless works of art, paintings, statues, bronzes, lithurgical ornaments, tapestries, furniture, chandeliers and candelabra, fabrics, embroidery, carpets and many other things which make of this palace one of the best, if not the very best, treasure chests in Spain.

When Napoleon walked up the great staircase of his brother Joseph's future residence with him, he felt obliged to say, «Joseph, tu serais mieux logé que moi». Among other things, this palace is truly unique for the quantity and the quality of its vaults, painted *al fresco,* and this for two reasons —first, because the 18th century marks the peak of interest in this sumptuary style of decoration and, secondly, because this new palace was constructed with vaults in brick or stone for fear of another fire like that in the memory of all. This vaulted construtcion brought with it extremely thick walls, giving strength to the palace, and made it necessary to decorate the vaults in the most noble and appropriate way.

Many took part in this enterprise —Giovanni Bautista Tiepolo (the best fresco painter of the time), Dominici Tiepolo, Corrado Giaquinto, Mengs, Salvador Maella, Bayeu, Alejandro González Velázquez, Vicente López... At the time no better constellation existed around the two main stars of Tiepolo and Giaquinto. This is so true that Francisco José Fabre wrote a book called *Descripción de las Alegorías pintadas en las bóvedas del Real Palacio de Madrid,* which was published in

65. *Alfonso XIII's private office. (Photograph by courtesy of the National Heritage).*

Madrid in 1829 by Eusebio Aguado, His Majesty's printer.

But in the present book one of the greatest difficulties has been that of summarising and choosing among all the things contained in this huge Aladin's cave —the Royal Palace in Madrid. For this reason we hope that the reader will forgive any grave omissions that may have ocurred to the benefit of less important references, but, as mentioned above, we have tried to include everything, yet at the same time avoid a cold inventory which would have detracted from the basic objective of this work —that of obtaining a vision of the whole that is both all-embracing and expressive.

66. *Exhibit in the collection of tapestries (Photograph by courtesy of the National Heritage).*

MUSEUMS AND COLLECTIONS

Apart from the palace in itself being a museum, as has been made clear in the previous chapters, there are within it a series of specific museums, collections and sections which are of great cultural interest. The collection of tapestries, that of musical instruments, that of carriages, that of medals and coins, the Royal Pharmacy and, above all, the Royal Armoury are real museums, some of them with priceless exhibits.

The collection of paintings is far inferior to that formerly housed in the palace, which, as is well known, was given away by Fernando VII to establish the Prado Museum. But although the collection in the Prado Museum was the real royal collection, there are nevertheless very fine paintings in the palace, which have been described under the section on the rooms on the main floor.

67. *Exhibit in the collection of tapestries (Photograph by courtesy of the National Heritage).*

68. *Exhibit in the collection of tapestries (Photograph by courtesy of the National Heritage).*

69. *Two exhibits in the collection of medals and coins*
(Photograph by courtesy of the National Heritage).

The number of tapestries in the National Heritage is so great that a new, real Tapestry Museum should be set up outside the Royal Palace. It has been suggested that this museum could be built on the grounds west of the La Almudena Cathedral, since they belong to the National Heritage. It is not known when work on this will begin, but it is obviously a pressing necessity.

The present exhibition of the collection of tapestries in the palace goes only a short way to solving the problem, as it has been calculated that there are some 1 200 belonging to the National Heritage, only a small number of which can be seen here, and a few more in the palace in La Granja.

The palace in Madrid houses some important tapestries, such as those from the series of *The Triumph of the Mother of God*, also known as *The Series of the Golden Hangings,* which are 15th century Flemish works.

Also very important are those belonging to *The John the Baptist Series,* after cartoons by Van Orley, stitched in Brussels in the 16th century. The *Descent of Christ* from the Cross, stitched in gold, is a fine 16th century piece from Brussels. There are also some 18th century French tapestries, such as that of Niove inducing the people to refuse to make offerings to Latona.

The *Story of David and Bathsheba* is a series of beautiful hangings made in Brussels in the 16th century. The oldest tapestry is exhibited in the small room called the Oratory. Late 15th century, Gothic in style, it depicts the *Birth of Jesus.* The small collection on show is very valuable, but far less than it could be if we consider what the National Heritage in fact possesses.

The *collections of medals and coins* are not only interesting, but also comprise a wealth of historic importance. Of particular interest in the royal col-

70. *The Royal Armoury. Jousting and battle armour
(Photograph by courtesy of the National Heritage).*

lection are the medals commemorating certain people in history, who were celebrated through these special mints. Of great importance is the collection made by Maria Christina of Hapsburg and Lorraine, mother of Alfonso XIII. Owing to her links with the House of Austria she received a considerable number of coins, on which she was very keen.

In addition, and now in a different realm of things, there is a fine *collection of musical instruments* in the palace, in particular the really extraordinary number of *Stradivarius* violins, perhaps the greatest indication of the musical brilliance of the court of Spain.

The collections of silver and porcelain, together with pieces from those of medals, coins and musical instruments are soon to be exhibited on the main floor, in the rooms adjoining the Banqueting Room.

The Royal Armoury is famous throughout the world. It is now situated in a huge room in *Armería Real* Square, in the buildings constructed during the last century to finish closing the square. In a very large room lined with glass showcases, decorated with beautiful tapestries and full of armour in a standing position or on horseback, there is one of the best collections of military armour in the world. Within this vast exhibition room you seem to be able to relive all the exploits of the mediaeval and Renaissance knights at their greatest moments. Here we cannot possibly stop to describe even the

71. *The distillation room in the Royal Pharmacy (Photograph by courtesy of the National Heritage).*

72. *The Royal Pharmacy Museum (Photograph by courtesy of the National Heritage).*

73. *The Carriage Museum. Ceremonial berlin, called «the shell coach», late 18th century. (Photograph by courtesy of the National Heritage).*

most important pieces in this collection, as it would need a separate catalogue to offer a mere summary of the main pieces, the schools to which they belong, the most important items, and who wore them in battles or tournaments. Much of the armour belonged to Arab kings, other pieces to famous captains such as Gonzalo de Córdoba and yet others to the kings of Spain, in particular to those of the House of Austria, who had armour made by the best craftsmen in Italy, Germany and Spain.

There are some very fine pieces, such as Emperor Carlos V's equestrian armour and German war trappings, as painted by Titian in 1548, after the victory in the battle of Mühlberg.

Not all the pieces can be mentioned here, but there is Roman-style armour, such as that by Bartolomé Carpi for Carlos V, and other pieces with short Gothic skirts, which are both stylish and military in appearance. The armoury of the Duke of Osuna was taken over by the Royal Armoury after the ruin of this noble family.

The PHARMACY, also siuated in one of the corridors on the side of Armería Square, is very interesting. Dating mainly from the times of Carlos IV, it contains installations from other periods as well, such as the distillation rooms, which are very old. Most of the bottles date from the Carlos IV period, although there are earlier examples —beautiful blue and white earthenware jars and pots from Talavera de la

74. *Road coach. The Carriage Museum (Photograph by courtesy of the National Heritage).*

Reina, as well as some later examples from the times of Alfonso XII. Nowadays, with so many of the traditional pharmacies disappearing, these are a fine testimony to the organisation of the old laboratories and depositories of curative medicines.

The most common item among these pharmaceutical implements are jars from the Royal Glass Workshop in La Granja and vials from the same place.

The CARRIAGE MUSEUM, which was opened in 1967, contains examples of all the most important 17th, 18th and 19th century vehicles. These carriages previously stood in a large coach house adjoining the royal stables, built by Sabatini in Bailén Street, together with an immense wealth of livery, harnesses, uniforms, horse trappings and magnificent decorations belonging to the royal entourage.

The stables in Bailén Street offered a fine exhibition of the whole fleet of royal vehicles, but this is now extremely reduced. However, what can be seen are the very best examples, such as a late 17th century carriage known as the *black one,* and a ceremonial berlin with bronze decorations, made in Madrid in 1832.

In this museum you can see the king's carriage, with its harnesses and life-size models of its grooms, postilions and coach drivers. Simpler, more everyday carriages such as *landaus, barouches* and *calashes* stand beside road coaches prepared for long journeys.

THE LIBRARY AND THE ARCHIVES

One very important element —the library and the archives— has been left to the end of this discussion of the cultural aspect of the palace. It is strange that in this palace the library was not designed with fine architecture and a magnificent setting. The library in the Royal Palace is very meritorious, but it lacks the monumentality of, for example, the library in El Escorial Monastery or certain libraries in palaces abroad, such as the magnificent one in the Imperial Palace in Vienna, by Fisher von Erlach. The library in the Royal Palace in Madrid is not of this kind —it is severe, sober and magnificently furnished, but it is of no architectural importance. It is lined with mahogany bookcases and large drawers (many of which stand in the centre of the rooms) containing maps, engravings and other types of documents.

The library contains very important collections, some of which are unique. These include manuscripts, incunabula, and old books and special materials such as drawings, engravings, photographs, music and maps.

Invaluable documentation for historical and literary studies (including collections of songs and poems, diverse plays, correspondence from Cardinal Granvela and papers belonging to the Count of Gondomar) can be seen, as well as pieces of unique artistic beauty, such as the Book of Hours with the arms of the Enríquez family, known as the *Libro de las Horas de Isabel la Católica,* Taccoli's *Teatro Militar,* Alfonso XI's *El Libro de la Montería,* as well as manuscripts about South America such as the *Códice Veitia,* one by Fray Bernardino de Sahagún and another called Trujillo de Perú by Martínez Compañón, which contains a wealth of amazing illustrations.

The variety of the collections makes of this library an indispensable reference centre for many branches of investigation. From the point of view of the actual history of books, the royal collection is one of the most interesting, and those studying bookbinding will find this an unequalled source, especially in Spanish rococo, neoclassical and Romantic binding (although there are also fine examples of 15th century Mudéjar as well as 16th and 17th century books). The collection also contains many works from the rest of Europe, particularly France.

Also of interest are the ARCHIVES. As Conrado Morterero says when speaking of the palace general archives in his book published by the National Heritage in 1975, both King José I Bonaparte and King Fernando VII should be congratulated on the creation of these archives. The former had the idea of collecting together all the documents relating to the staff in the estates belonging to the royal family and those from the administrators of these estates. Then Fernando VII, after his return from Valenzay in 1814, set to organising the archives, because he felt an urgent need to arrange his house so as to know the rights of the Royal Heritage and to determine the expenses of the royal family which, as they were combined with those of the Treasury, were completely uncontrolled and allowed no fixed sum. In this way the first steps towards the documentation of the royal household and heritage, now the General Archives of the National Heritage, were taken.

75. *Miniatures from a Book of Hours in the palace library (Photograph by courtesy of the National Heritage).* ▶

ao completri

The present archives were preceded by those considered private archives of the comptroller's and the greffier's offices, originally in the old court of Burgundy. We shall not enter into details here, as it is not the right place, of what exactly the comptroller and the greffier did, except to say that they were responsible for the accounts of everything relating to *His Royal Highness,* to the king.

All this paperwork led to an accumulation of documents which over the years became fundamental to the understanding of the history of Spain, and, in particular, of its monarchy. These documents are now conserved in the archives, situated in the low building that closes Armería Square, between the palace and the armoury.

The archives also contain documents which are very important for the history of Art, particularly those concerning the Council for Public Works and Woods, as well as those about the castles and other buildings belonging to the royal family. There are many notes containing the names of artists such as Velázquez (his appointment as master of the palace is kept here), and later messages referring to Sachetti, Sabatini, Mengs, Gasparini and Goya.

The archives have been greatly improved recently with regard to the installations and space, the organisation of registers, the new cases for the conservation of old papers, and so on. In fact, because of the latest work carried out the archives now are distributed over three spacious floors of continuous galleries with three of them on the lower ground floor and five in the basement. Part of the middle floor is used for storerooms and the rest is given over to offices, toilets and research rooms.

Altogether, the collections occupy 11 km of shelves with 25 000 bundles of papers, 24 000 cases, 12 000 registers and over six thousand plans and drawings.

76. *The Campo del Moro Gardens.*

AROUND THE PALACE:
OTHER PROJECTS AND BUILDINGS

Unlike other European palaces, this was not fortunate in the construction of further buildings to provide an interesting monumental environment to match it harmoniously. The building of the palace was so extraordinarily expensive, because of the type of stone building, because of the grandeur and quality of the materials used and because of its ornamentation (which was, unfortunately, more or less simplified later), that there was neither time nor enough money to complete the palace with a setting worthy of its grandeur. It should also be remembered that the death of

Carlos III meant the loss of the driving force behind all that in Madrid was grandeur, monumental constructions and the embellishment of public places. But even before then it had been impossible to carry out some projects by Sachetti and Sabatini which were really so vast and so lavish that not even Carlos III, whose life, like that of all mortals, had its limits, could attempt them.

Carlos IV's reign was completely different from that of his father's. Problems built up, there was a crisis in the country, and finally the French Revolu-

77. *A pond in the Campo del Moro Gardens.*

tion brought great unrest and instability to the courts of Europe, which later also suffered during the difficult Napoleonic period.

Because of this, the great palace in Madrid stood alone, with no important retinue of buildings to attest to it. It could in fact be said that nothing was done around the palace except knock things down. Joseph Bonaparte, the intruder king, who hazardously ruled in Madrid for a short period, mainly demolished old buildings, some of them interesting churches, in order to construct, perhaps with his great architect Silvestre Pérez, the buildings to stand around the palace. But in the end, the *little square king,* as he was known (for

72

78. *Detail of the Shell Fountain.*

79. *View of the Campo del Moro Gardens. In the background, the Shell Fountain.*

80. *The Tritons Fountain.*

opening up a series of spaces in which to create squares) was only able to do this negative piece of work, without ever beginning to construct anything interesting. The best idea his architect Silvestre Pérez had was that· of joining the palace with the church of San Francisco el Grande by means of a monumental bridge, later to become the viaduct, but because of the hazardous nature of Joseph Napoleon's reign nothing ever came of it.

When Fernando VII came to the throne after the War of Independence he encountered a country in a situation of almost complete ruin, bound both hand and foot. He had a great architect —Isidro González Velázquez— but although this man made an interesting project for Oriente Square he was not even able to begin it, and a modest version of what he had imagined was built. In short, the palace remained alone.

There followed the reign of Isabel II, during which Armería Square was completed (well, something is better than nothing) and the Campo del Moro Gardens were finally laid out —in English style, quite different from the baroque gardens which would have suited the palace. But this was a positive step, and a beautiful avenue with two fountains was opened up through the palace park. Called the *Tritons* and the *Shell Fountains* they added solemnity and grandeur to the gardens.

81. *The cork pavilion in the Campo del Moro Gardens.*

Let us take another step forwards into the times of the 2nd Republic, and just when it seemed that things were not going to change the local council came up with the idea of knocking down the old stables and the large carriage-house to the north of the palace and creating gardens there. The demolition of the carriage house was of no great importance, but that of the stables, a fine construction by Sabatini, was a serious loss. The same gardens could have been cre-

82. *The Queen's House in the Campo del Moro Gardens.*

83. *The Palace from the Campo del Moro Gardens.* ▶

ated retaining part of the stables, thus blocking the new gardens off from the brow of San Vicente Hill, which is hardly an interesting background for the palace grounds. These gardens were laid out following plans by Fernando García Mercadal, and it is only fair to acknowledge that his layout, with the organisation of the flower beds and the position of the large pond, that sheet of water which reflects the north façade of the palace, is absolutely perfect.

Another loss suffered by the palace and its dependent buildings has been that of not extending the Senate with a building that would lengthen the façade of Sabatini's former Council of State. In this way, a set of buildings coherent with the Royal Palace would have been achieved.

Finally, there was, unfortunately, an unfinished building beside the palace, which was the new *La Almudena Cathedral*. This cathedral was begun by the architect Francisco de Cubas, the Marquis of Cubas, in a neo-Gothic style which was not at all in keeping with the baroque-classicist palace built by Sachetti and Sabatini. But in the end, though it is not really my place to comment on this, the situation was changed with the development of a new project which has not demolished any of the Gothic work begun by the Marquis of Cubas but has enveloped his mediaeval structure in a classicist cloak that respects the Royal Palace.

When the La Almudena Cathedral is finished, not only will a fine religious building have been constructed, but also the palace will certainly have gained what it has very gradually been striving for —a dignified environment worthy of its grandeur.

84. *La Almudena Cathedral.*

INDEX

THE SPANISH NATIONAL HERITAGE COLLECTION

El Escorial
Los Caídos Valley
The Convent of Santa Maria La Real de Huelgas
The Royal Palace in Madrid
La Almudaina Palace